OUR PLANET

Volcanoes
and
Earthquakes

ZUZA VRBOVA

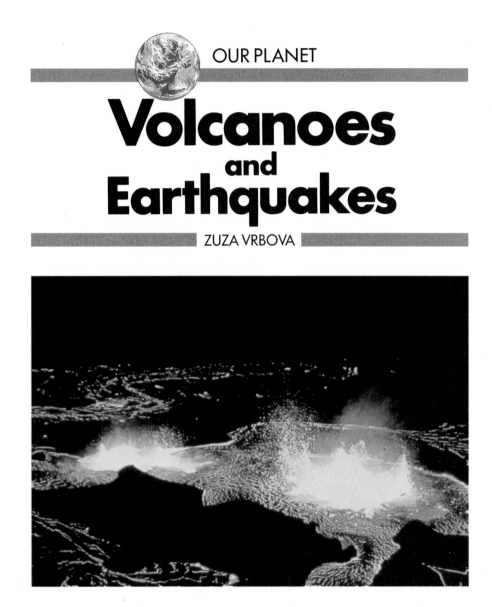

Troll Associates

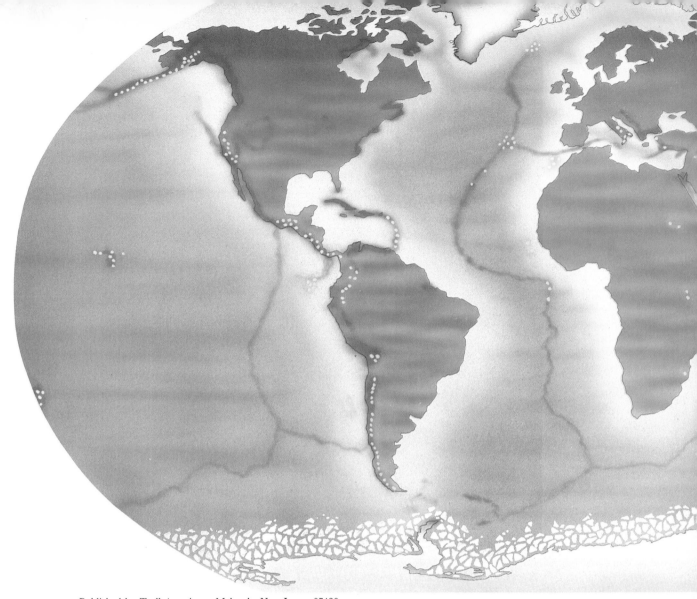

Published by Troll Associates, Mahwah, New Jersey 07430

Design by James Marks, London.
Picture research by Jan Croot.
Illustrators: Martin Camm: pages 20, 21, 22-23, 26, 27; Chris Forsey: page 14; Sebastian Quigley: pages 6-7, 10, 13, 16, 19, 24; Mike Roffe: pages 8-9, 28-29; Paul Sullivan: pages 12-13; Ian Thompson: pages 2-3.
Printed in the U.S.A.
10 9 8 7 6 5 4 3 2 1

Library of Congress Cataloging-in-Publication Data

Vrbova, Zuza.
    Volcanoes & earthquakes / by Zuza Vrbova; illustrated by Michael Roffe, Paul Sullivan, & Ian Thompson.
        p.   cm.—(Our planet)
    Summary: Discusses how and where volcanoes and earthquakes occur and other aspects of these disturbances in the earth.
    ISBN 0-8167-1977-2 (lib. bdg.)   ISBN 0-8167-1978-0 (pbk.)
    1. Volcanoes—Juvenile literature.   2. Earthquakes—Juvenile literature. [1. Volcanoes. 2. Earthquakes] I. Roffe, Michael, ill.
II. Sullivan, Paul, ill. III. Thompson, Ian, ill. IV. Title.
V. Title: Volcanoes and earthquakes. VI. Series.
QE521.3.V73   1990
551.2′1—dc20   89-20334

Map: Volcanoes (yellow dots)
Earthquakes and plate
boundaries (purple)

Title page:
Lava lake in Hawaii

CONTENTS

Volcanoes in Action

The Earth's surface is made of solid rocks. But beneath the surface, in the inner Earth, the rocks are so hot that they are in a liquid, or *molten*, state. Molten rock contains gases that are always expanding or exploding. They need to escape. Volcanoes are the openings in the Earth's surface through which these rocks and gases burst.

Around the world, some 800 volcanoes are *active*, erupting regularly. Others are seemingly quiet, or *dormant*, but could erupt or explode at any time. *Extinct* volcanoes are those that have ceased all activity. "Dormant" comes from the Latin word for "sleeping," and sometimes dormant volcanoes are mistakenly thought to be extinct.

↑ Molten rocks and gases sometimes escape to the surface of the Earth through a vent in the side of a volcano. Glowing clouds of hot gas and ash are produced as steam and lava pour from the vent.

→ The shape of a volcano depends on the way it erupts. Volcanoes that erupt explosively **(left)**, such as Vesuvius in Italy, are shaped like cones. This shape is formed by the piling up of layer upon layer of lava. The Hawaiian kind of volcano **(middle)** has a very wide base, and runny lava gently seeps out. These volcanoes sometimes grow from vents in the ocean floor. The most violent volcanoes **(right)**, like Mount Saint Helens in the U.S., are caused by the explosive release of molten rock from deep down in the Earth.

4

↑ Fire fountains on Mount Etna, on the large Italian island of Sicily. Etna's first recorded eruption was in 476 B.C., and the volcano is still active. It has a central vent and over 200 smaller openings.

5

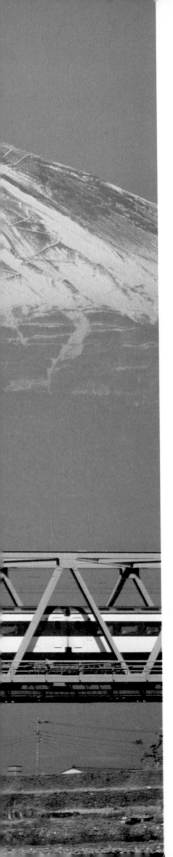

Millions of years ago, there were volcanoes in all parts of the world. Traces of them still exist — in New York State, England, and Australia, for example. Edinburgh Castle, in Scotland, is built on a volcano that has been extinct for 325 million years.

Volcanoes are mostly found in mountainous regions and under the oceans. The ones flanking the Pacific Ocean are known as the "Ring of Fire." Their perfect cone-shaped peaks poke out above the warm, flat sea. Some have been quiet for centuries, while others send out delicate wisps of steam. But if the steam turns to angry clouds and rumbles and muffled explosions begin deep underground, these are warning signals that the volcano will erupt. Still, nothing further may happen for years. Then, suddenly, enormous fountains of burning rock spout through the volcano's central *vent*, or hole. Such eruptions are often accompanied by earthquakes and violent lightning storms.

The liveliest volcanoes continually pour out a frothing stream of molten or liquid rock known as *lava*. Tourists often climb Mount Etna, Europe's largest volcano, to watch the fireworks at its vent. But volcanoes do the unexpected, and in 1872 a group of tourists was so absorbed by the spectacle that it was engulfed by a stream of red-hot lava.

We associate volcanoes with death and destruction, but people live near them because they produce wonderful farming land. The gases and rocks they spew out also help us to understand the workings of the inner Earth.

← Mount Fuji, in Japan, is a dormant volcano. It last erupted in 1707.

Volcanic Islands

Exploding islands have caused some of the most terrifying disasters in history. Santorini, a large island in the Aegean Sea, was torn apart by a volcanic eruption in 1470 B.C. Once it was a center of the great Minoan civilization. Today it is a tiny island with beaches of black volcanic sand and a steep, unnatural-looking coast.

The volcano on Krakatoa, an island in the Indian Ocean, remained quiet for centuries. But in 1883 four massive explosions which could be heard 2,000 miles away destroyed it. The island was not blasted into the air. The top of the volcano was undermined and sank beneath the waves, causing *tsunamis*. These are gigantic waves that can travel at up to 500 miles per hour. They are often wrongly called tidal waves. As the tsunamis from Krakatoa hit the neighboring shores of Java and Sumatra, more than 36,000 people were drowned.

New volcanic islands seem to appear from nowhere. In 1927, a small volcanic island named Anak Krakatoa ("Child of Krakatoa") suddenly surfaced where Krakatoa had been. If you sail through the Straits of Java, you can see an orange glow from dozens of small volcanoes lighting the sky at night.

The explosion of Krakatoa was so huge that it destroyed part of the volcano and sent a cloud of ash and dust around the world (**left**). All that was left of the three-coned island was a huge crater, stretching 920 feet below sea level. Anak Krakatoa, a small active volcano, has now grown in its place (**right**).

↑ The volcanic island of Surtsey rising from the Atlantic Ocean in 1963. It was formed by an underwater volcanic eruption. A massive cloud of steam rose from the island as sea rushed into the volcano's vent.

In 1963, fishermen near the coast of Iceland watched in amazement as the sea started to boil. Slowly a black cone shape rose from the waves. This new island was named Surtsey, after a legendary Icelandic giant.

Inside the Earth

The Earth was born out of a hot, swirling mass of gases and dust. As it cooled, it solidified into a sphere made up of layers. The outermost layer, the *atmosphere*, still consists entirely of gases. But the surface layers are made of rock.

The Earth's outer surface is its *crust*. If the Earth were an apple, the crust would be no thicker than the apple's skin.

But, unlike an apple skin, the crust is not a continuous surface. It consists of a jigsaw of continents and ocean floors resting on a layer of rock called the *mantle*. In places where the crust is broken, part of the upper mantle can melt and form *magma*, or molten rock. When magma is forced through the crust, it flows out of volcanoes as lava. Beneath the mantle, the Earth has an *outer core*, probably made of molten iron, and, at the very center, an *inner core*, which is mainly solid iron.

↓ Volcanoes and earthquakes are a reminder that the Earth's surface is constantly in motion. It is made up of plates of rock, which move around. Most volcanoes are caused by plate movements. Volcanoes form when two plates meet or move apart, or when the edge of one plate is pushed under another. There are a few volcanoes that are far from plate edges, but lie directly above hot spots in the Earth's mantle.

Moving Continents

The pieces of the jigsaw that make up the Earth's crust are called *plates*. There are six major plates and several minor ones. Some are the continents, others the ocean floors. Each plate is an immense area of rock about 20 miles thick. Slowly they are being moved about by currents of soft, hot rock deep inside the Earth. But the few inches they move each year are only noticeable in photos taken by satellites.

Did you know that the land occupied by the Sahara Desert was once where the South Pole is now? Over millions of years, our world map is being altered. However, these movements put enormous pressure on the surface rock. When two continental plates collide, the rocks at their edges buckle. This is how the Himalayas were formed.

↑ The Earth's crust is divided into plates. The dotted lines show the boundaries between plates. Some plates form the continents, others the ocean floors.

When an oceanic plate collides with a continental plate, it is forced underneath it. As the cooler rock of the oceanic plate sinks into the red-hot magma below, the reaction is violent. The Earth is shaken by earthquakes, and volcanoes burst into life. Examples of mountains formed in this way are the Cascade Range in North America and the Andes of South America.

→ Near Pingvellir, in Iceland, you can clearly see where the European and North American plates meet. A major earthquake occurred here in 1789.

Volcanoes Under the Sea

The ocean floor is believed to be spreading. A chain of underwater mountains, 40,000 miles long and several hundred miles wide, runs along the sea bed. It is known as the *mid-ocean ridge*. Cracks in the ridge are widened by lava welling up from the inner Earth. This pushes the ocean floor apart. Some of the lava plugs the surface, and some piles up vertically, forming cone-shaped volcanic islands.

Certain peaks of the mid-ocean ridge rise 20,000 feet or more above the sea bed, making it the world's greatest mountain range. The highest peak is Mauna Kea, a volcano in Hawaii. It is 33,000 feet high, and more than half its height is hidden in the ocean depths.

The Earth is not getting bigger. While some oceans are spreading, the Pacific is gradually shrinking. Once the Mediterranean was a large ocean. Now it is a sea. Eventually, as the plates close up, it will disappear and be replaced by a mountain range.

Each year there are more than a million underwater earthquakes. Most are so small they go unnoticed, but about every two weeks a more violent tremor shakes the ocean floor.

← In Hawaii, you can often see flames and steam rising from the lava in the sea. Hawaii is made up of a chain of over 20 volcanic islands in the Pacific Ocean.

↓ Red-hot magma is constantly seeping out from cracks in the Earth's crust onto the ocean floor. The cracks appear where two plates meet, and the magma forms ridges as it cools and hardens. This volcanic activity is slowly widening some oceans. Sometimes magma piles up to make underwater volcanoes. Some of these eventually become islands. There are also deep trenches in the oceans where rock is destroyed by two plates pushing against each other. This makes the edge of one plate slip underneath the other. As the plate descends into the hot mantle, it melts to form magma. Some of the magma rises up through the plate and reaches the surface of the sea bed through volcanic vents.

Land of Fire and Ice

Iceland's landscape was sculpted by fire and ice. It is an island of broken lava surfaces, cone-shaped mountains, and deserts of black sand. Jutting out above the icy Atlantic waters, it is a part of the oceanic ridge. Iceland was formed by lava oozing out of a *rift*, or crack, in the ocean floor. "Gentle" eruptions of this kind frequently occur where two oceanic plates are moving apart. Layer upon layer of lava cools and hardens into an island of dark gray rock. Known as *basalt*, this is the most common type of volcanic rock.

The drift ice piled onto its coastline by the cold Atlantic currents gives Iceland its name. About one eighth of the island is covered by glaciers. The winter snows seldom melt, but under Iceland volcanic fires still burn. Water heated by molten rock deep underground bubbles up as hot springs, or gushes high into the air as steaming fountains called *geysers*. Water from hot springs is piped directly into people's homes. Naturally heated swimming pools are used for open-air bathing even in midwinter.

For 5,400 years, the Helgafell volcano was dormant, but in 1973 a huge crack opened up on its slopes. Lava threatened the 5,000 inhabitants of Vestmannaeyjar, the fishing port nearby. But by hastily building barriers of volcanic ash, they managed to direct the flowing lava safely into the sea.

← Helgafell erupting in 1973. Red-hot lava streamed from the volcano, threatening the fishing port below. Volunteers remained in the town to save it from being buried in lava and to clear burning ash from the houses.

↓ Geysers shoot hot water and steam into the air, and can reach heights of more than 400 feet. They occur when water is heated by molten rock deep underground and forces its way up to the Earth's surface.

17

Hawaiian Hot Spot

Unlike most other volcanoes, the Hawaiian Islands were created not by plates colliding or separating but by an unusually hot area deep in the Earth's mantle. Volcanoes are formed above a *hot spot* when a surge of magma pierces the ocean floor. Eventually plate movement carries them away from the hot spot, and they then become extinct. In this way, a chain of islands is created, with active volcanoes in the middle and extinct ones beyond the hot-spot region.

Mauna Kea is a Hawaiian volcano that moved away from the hot spot. If measured from its base on the sea bed to its summit towering above the Pacific Ocean, it is the world's tallest mountain. It is also the best place in the Northern Hemisphere for observing stars. Now Mauna Loa, the world's second tallest mountain, lies above the hot spot and spurts out lava and flames.

Before an eruption, a volcano swells as magma wells up inside it, and earth tremors often increase. By watching for signs such as these, scientists have predicted a number of eruptions in Hawaii in time to move people to safety.

← The Hawaiian island
volcanoes were formed above a
hot spot when magma pierced
the Pacific plate. The plate is
slowly moving, as shown by the
white arrow. Over millions of
years, as the plate moves, a
new volcanic island forms. The
newest active volcano is directly
above the hot spot. The volcano
on the right has moved away
and become extinct.

↑ The Hawaiian chain of
volcanic islands stretches for
1,500 miles across the central
Pacific Ocean. Eruptions in
Hawaii can be spectacular, with
fountains of orange-colored
flames and lava spurting directly
from the sea.

The Cascades

When Mount Saint Helens exploded in 1980, it released as much energy as 500 Hiroshima-type atomic bombs. It had been dormant for 123 years, and its reawakening came with terrible suddenness. Weeks later, a cloud of gas and white-hot ash was still drifting over the states of Washington and Idaho.

Such violence is typical of volcanic explosions that happen at the point where two plates collide. Lava from these volcanoes does not flow freely. It is squeezed slowly through the rocks like glue from a tube, only flowing a short distance before it hardens. Sometimes it solidifies inside the volcano, forming a *plug* that blocks the vent. If pressure continues to build up below, it can only be released by a huge explosion. Not only the plug but half the mountain may be blown away.

↑ Crater Lake, Oregon. The lake is encircled by the Cascade Mountains. Near the shore, a small volcanic island rises from the lake.

Like Mount Saint Helens, Crater Lake is part of the Cascade Range. It is the deepest lake in North America. Having no inlet or outlet, it is kept full by rain and snow. It lies in the crater created by the explosion of an ancient volcano named Mazama. The force of the explosion was so powerful that the crater is 6 miles across.

← Ash and gases shooting out of Mount Saint Helens during the eruption in 1980. Mount Saint Helens is 9,671 feet high and is part of the Cascade Range.

21

Buried Cities

For almost 2,000 years, the Roman city of Pompeii in southern Italy lay buried under a layer of volcanic ash more than 13 feet deep. In 1748, the King of Sicily ordered the city to be dug free. What the workers uncovered has told us much about the way the Romans lived. Houses, shops, and restaurants were preserved exactly as they were on the day Vesuvius exploded in A.D.79. There were even perfect imprints of a tethered dog and an unfinished meal.

Life came to an instant halt that day. Pompeii had been a wealthy seaside city with 20,000 inhabitants. More than 2,000 were killed in the sudden explosion. Others were suffocated by the huge cloud of poisonous gas and ash that hung over the city for weeks. Because the falling ash was mixed with steam, it became as hard as concrete.

The Romans had mistakenly thought that Vesuvius was an extinct volcano, although 17 years earlier an earthquake had destroyed parts of Pompeii and the neighboring town of Herculaneum. But deep in the ground beneath them, the Earth was renewing its activity. While they were busy repairing the earlier damage to their cities, Vesuvius struck again.

Herculaneum was also buried, under a sea of mud, ash, and lava up to 100 feet deep. But the people there had more time to escape. In both cities, furniture, paintings, jewelry, tools, and other objects have been beautifully preserved.

22

← Plaster casts of a tethered dog and a dead man. Bodies were covered by layers of ash. In time flesh and clothing decayed, leaving only bones. Lifelike models have been made by pumping plaster into the hollows around the bones.

↑ Pompeii as it is today, with Mount Vesuvius in the background. When the great eruption came, most of these buildings were already in ruins after the earthquake 17 years earlier. Vesuvius last erupted in 1944.

23

↑ A tsunami near Anak Krakatoa, a volcanic island in Indonesia. The wave is so high that the volcano is only just visible. Tsunamis can travel at up to 500 miles per hour.

→ As a tsunami takes about ten hours to travel from Japan to Hawaii, a Pacific warning system has been set up to tell people of the coming danger. Many lives have been saved by moving people from villages in the path of an oncoming tsunami.

Forecasting Earthquakes

If you bend a plastic ruler far enough, it will break. The Earth's crust is being bent in a similar fashion by forces we don't fully understand. When it reaches the breaking point, we experience earthquakes. As the ground vibrates, homes, buildings, bridges, and dams can collapse like a stack of cards. But people are killed by the effects rather than the cause.

The more we understand earthquakes, the better we can protect ourselves against them. Most of the damage they do is caused by faulty construction. Engineers now know how to construct buildings that can withstand most earthquakes. Panic is another common cause of death. As people rush into the streets, they are crushed by falling debris or by stumbling over one another.

When the Earth's crust breaks, it sends out shock waves. Known as *seismic waves* (from the Greek word for "shake"), these make the Earth tremble. In the ocean, they become *tsunamis*. Tsunami is the Japanese word for "harbor wave." They are called this because as the sea becomes shallower near the coast, the waves become taller. Drop a stone in a river and watch the ripples. The effect is similar to the pattern created by tsunamis and seismic waves.

Seismologists, scientists who study earthquakes, monitor the Earth's movements with a *seismograph*. Large earthquakes are often preceded by small shocks, and this instrument can measure even the smallest tremors. By discovering more about the patterns of the Earth's movements, seismologists are now learning how to predict earthquakes.

San Andreas Fault

In 1906, San Francisco was rocked by a terrible earthquake. For three days afterward a fire raged through the city. Much of San Francisco was destroyed and many lives were lost. Rebuilding began almost immediately, but the city has suffered from more recent tremors, including a major earthquake in 1989.

↑ Ancient Chinese earthquake detector. An earth tremor moves a pendulum inside, which makes the balls fall from the dragons' teeth into the mouths of the frogs waiting below.

San Francisco lies on the San Andreas Fault, a large crack in the Earth's surface running from the Gulf of California to the coast north of San Francisco. Here the plate carrying the North American continent meets the plate supporting the Pacific Ocean and its floor.

The Pacific plate is grinding its way northward at an average rate of 2 inches a year. Some 12 miles below the surface it moves easily because the rock is molten. But at the level of the solid crust, rock grinds against rock. A kink on the plate can cause it to stick. Pressure then builds up, as the molten rock keeps on pushing, until the crust jerks free.

Seismologists check the fault daily, using all kinds of equipment. So many people live in the area that advance warning of a major earthquake is vital.

← Advance warning of an earthquake can save many lives. *Creepmeters* placed along parts of the fault line record the slightest rock movements. *Lasers* are also used to monitor movements of the Earth's crust.

Magnetometers measure changes in the magnetic properties of cracked rocks. All this information is transmitted to laboratories by satellite.

↑ Cars crushed by a collapsing building during an earthquake that shook Los Angeles in 1987. Los Angeles lies to the east of the San Andreas Fault.

Other Planets

Space probes have discovered volcanoes on other planets. Mars has several, all extinct. Of these, Olympus is the largest in the solar system. It is nearly three times as high as Mount Everest, the Earth's highest peak. At its base it is 370 miles across, and its crater is 40 miles wide.

Venus also has giant volcanoes, created by hot spots deep below its surface. Maxwell, the tallest, is over a mile higher than Everest. It is thought to be extinct, but other Venusian volcanoes, such as Rhea and Theia, erupt continuously. Lightning storms rage around them as they pour out clouds of gas into the flame-colored sky.

Even more spectacular are the volcanoes on Io, one of Jupiter's many moons. In 1979 the *Voyager* space probes photographed three of them, Pele, Prometheus, and Loki, blowing plumes of sulphur 100 miles into the sky.

The continual eruptions, lightning storms, and violent earthquakes on Venus and Io give a vivid idea of how the Earth must have looked billions of years ago, shortly after it was formed.

→ Sulphur plumes rise from volcanoes on Io. Another of Jupiter's moons is in the background. This painting is based on a *Voyager* photo.

↓ Extinct volcanoes on Mars. The planet has vast canyons and lava plains and giant volcanoes.

Fact File

Tallest Volcanoes
Measured from top to bottom, Mauna Kea in Hawaii is 33,000 feet high, but only the top 14,000 feet stand out above the sea.

The tallest volcanoes on land are:

Active: Ojos del Salado
   22,588 feet
Dormant: Llullaillaco
   22,109 feet
Extinct: Aconcagua
   22,834 feet

All three are in the Andes in South America.

Largest Crater
Lake Toba, a crater lake in Sumatra, Indonesia, has an area of 685 square miles.

Exploding Islands
It has been calculated that the explosion of Krakatoa in 1883 was as powerful as 25 nuclear bombs or 1,500 megatons of high explosives. The explosion of Santorini in 1470 B.C. is believed to have been five times as powerful as that of Krakatoa.

↓ *Lava plug at Le Puy, France*

Most Violent Eruptions
When Tambora in Sumbawa, Indonesia, erupted in 1815, it left a crater 7 miles wide and killed more than 90,000 people. The eruption was as powerful as 20,000 megatons of high explosives.

When Bezymianny in Russia erupted in 1956, it spurted out lava and ash at 1,500 feet per second (twice the speed of sound), scattering it 25 miles into the air.

Lucky Escape
In 1902, Mount Pelée, on the Caribbean island of Martinique, erupted, reducing the picturesque city of St. Pierre to ruins. Only two of St. Pierre's 30,000 inhabitants survived. One was a young shoemaker named Léon Compère-Léandre, who managed to run away from the city. The other, a convict named Auguste Ciparis, was having breakfast in a dungeon in the city jail.

Flowing Lava
Lava can advance as fast as 40 miles per hour, but it usually flows at no more than 10 miles per hour.
Lava stops flowing when it cools to about 1,200°F. The temperature of molten lava is usually between 1,500°F and 2,000°F.

Lava Plugs
You sometimes see steep-sided rocks called "lava plugs" towering above a plain or desert in an area where there are volcanoes. These are

formed when debris from an explosion hardens inside the vent of a volcano. Over thousands of years, wind and rain wear away the "walls" of the vent, until only the plug remains.

Most Powerful Geysers
The world's tallest active geyser is Steamboat Geyser in Yellowstone National Park, Wyoming. It has gushed out steaming water up to 380 feet into the air. Nearly all of the world's geysers are in three areas: Iceland, New Zealand, and Yellowstone Park.

↓ *Geyser in Yellowstone Park*

In 1904, the Waimangu geyser in New Zealand spurted out a fountain of water more than 1,500 feet high. However, it has not been active since 1917.

Volcano in a Cornfield
On February 20, 1943 a crack appeared in a cornfield in Mexico. This was the birth of a new volcano, named Paricutín. Within a week it grew 500 feet, and by February 1952 it was 1,350 feet high.

Measuring Earthquakes
Various methods are used for comparing the force of earthquakes. The best known

is the Richter scale, which measures the energy an earthquake releases. Most of the 1 million tremors that occur every year only reach 2 on the Richter scale. Those that reach 8 on the scale are powerful enough to flatten cities.

Earthquakes Since 1900
These earthquakes reached 8.5 or over on the Richter scale:

1906 Colombia coast, South
    America 8.6
1920 Kansu Province, China
    8.6
1950 Assam, India 8.6
1952 Kamchatka, U.S.S.R. 8.5
1964 Anchorage, Alaska 8.5

The 1906 San Francisco earthquake reached 8.3 on the Richter scale. The one which shook Mexico City in 1985 reached 8.1.

The earthquake in Armenia, U.S.S.R., in 1988 reached 6.9 on the Richter scale. Estimates of the number of people killed vary from 40,000 to 100,000.

↓ *Clearing debris after the 1988 Armenian earthquake*

Index